Lay My Burdens Down

The Spicy Truth of a Preacher's Kid

To Kate, Forgiveness is just the start and you have started a journey that you are so deserving of.

By Geneva N. Rambo

Please remember to love on Kate and to chose Kate first :)

your Therapist

Geneva Rambo

Kansas City, Missouri
geneva.rambo@gmail.com

First Edition, 2022

Geneva N. Rambo
Lay My Burdens Down
The Spicy Truth of a Preacher's Kid
Cover Photo: Unsplash Cristofer Maximilian
Cover design/manuscript editing: Natasha Ria El-Scari
Author photo: Terren Jones

ISBN: 9798443925905

Printed in the United States of America

Robert Theus V
December 12, 1993—May 25, 2020

Dedication

To My Dearest Son Robert Theus V,

I have so many thoughts, words, and emotions that I need to express, but for the sake of time I will just narrow it down. Robert, I knew you were something special from the moment I felt your presence inside of my womb. I remember the nurse standing over me during your sonogram when I was just four months pregnant. The nurse said jokingly, "Wow, look at this little joker jumping up and down." Even then son, you defied all the odds that were stacked against you. This makes me think of the time when your aunt snatched you out of my arms at six months old and said, "I am going to sweep his feet because he wants to walk!" I thought to myself, *there is no way in hell that this boy is going to walk so soon*, but four days later your little butt took off. You also defied the idea that only children were spoiled and selfish. Do not get me wrong, you were spoiled rotten, but you were kind. Growing up, I remember your ass giving away a brand-new pair of Jordans that you begged for without even asking my permission. My immediate reaction was to beat your "spoiled" ass, but the spirit loudly reminded me that I had raised a son who was giving and kind. I quickly changed my tone and wrapped my arms around you to let you know that God would always bless you for your kindness. From that moment forward, I knew that I had given birth to someone who would always have the heart of a cheerful giver. I love you son, and I always will!

Sincerely,

Your Mama

Acknowledgments

I would like to take the opportunity to thank everyone who was there for me for this part of my journey. For every tear, every call when I didn't expect it, this journey was like no other. I couldn't even see myself being two years from this tragedy but here I am.

Mommy, Daddy, thank you for being the example of all life's lessons.

Godmother, a woman of little words but they are always powerful.

All my grandchildren, I will forever ever be proud of what your father has left for me to oversee. I look at your pictures and cry because I see your Daddy in each of you. I will fiercely protect you with all that is in me.

To my sweet baby I know God blessed me with. The Father was intentional when he took one, he stepped in and replaced one with another, and it was you. I love you Diamond.

To LaTrice, you were chosen for a reason, Robert loved you and so do I. Keep smiling because we are going to the top.

Leon, my rock, who has just been there. Thank you for being by my side and for holding me up when no one else was there.

To my best friends who have been my best friends for decades: Tiffany, April, and Temaka. I want to thank each of you for the calls, for holding the phone for me, for everything.

I want to give a special shoutout to my two nieces, Rishawn and Terren for always making sure I am ok. They are intentional and consistent. They make things happen.

My cousin Kanika, my Batman to my Robin, you are my cousin-sister and have been with me every step of the way.

My sister Kathy, thank you so much for being my backbone. You are there for my sadness and my joy. We are conjoined in spirit.

Shout out to my cousin crew: Quiana, Kionna, Lerenda, Jameika, Brittanie, and Breonica! Thank you for all the times we've laughed, cried, done stupid stuff, came back and cried again.

I know the saying is blood is thicker than water but we must have water in order to survive. With that, to my sisters and brother, Ronnetta, Avadonn, Shonda, Karen, Devon and Mike.

To the most humble people I know: Julie, Sherry, Stacey, Erika and Martesha. I love you and thank you for loving me in return.

To my mother and father's personal care team: Ms. Boone, Tina Johnson and Yolanda Walters. I love you and I appreciate every moment you have dedicated to my parents.

Thank you to my family. I know when you read this your initial thought may be WOW but don't look at it with the wrong eyes, look at it with the right "I's". Let's get back to where we once were. It is definitely possible because God said so!

Disclaimer

Some names have been changed and/or omitted to protect the identity of those who may desire it. This book is an autobiography and is written from the perspective of how I experienced my life. It is not to replace or dismiss someone else's reality or truth.

A Letter to a Preachers' Kid

To All My Fellow Preachers' Kids,

I know that we have all heard the cliche that preachers' kids are the worst kids, but I detest that theory. In fact, preachers' kids are no different than police, teachers, or even children of politicians. We are expected to be different because of the calling that has been placed on our parents' lives. I am encouraging all preachers' kids to live in their truth. Continue to stand even when you feel weak, and speak boldly against wrongdoing because that is what God has ordained us to do. Above all, always remember to love. Love your family, love yourself, and most importantly continue to love God!

Sincerely,

Geneva Rambo

Table of Contents

Preface   1

Chapter 1: The Love Story that Started it All   12

Chapter 2: The Church   21

Chapter 3: The Final Straw   26

Chapter 4: The Family   38

Chapter 5: Butterfly   46

Chapter 6: Love is a Journey   51

Chapter 7: Address it!   65

Chapter 8: My Journey   68

About the Author   72

Preface

Imagine your whole life changing because of one single moment in time. A moment that imprinted on your heart and mind, which made you begin to question everything you have ever known...Now that I have begun, I think it would be best that I give a bit of background about who I am before I dive into sharing intricate details of my life. A crucial piece of information that is important to this literary journey is that you know that I am a preacher's kid. Anyone who knows me can attest that my entire existence was built around the church, and after a strenuous, spiritual journey I have concluded that the church has nothing to do with the building but has everything to do with the people who fill the building.

I will be very upfront and state that my truth may ruffle some feathers, but I ask that you think introspectively about why my truth may offend you. My truth is mine, and no matter what you feel after reading this I want you to know that this is my way to lay down every burden that has ever taken a toll on my life. Over the years, I have reaped the benefits of my family name, my entire family has but it was something that came with the territory. I will be transparent and let you know that it was not as pompous as you might think. The benefits came with pain, bitterness, and rage to say the least. I have accepted the circumstances, and have since been able to find healing, peace, and purpose through it all. Please know that the stories that I am about to tell are based solely upon events that have happened to me or I have directly witnessed throughout my life.

Disclaimer; this journey may make you laugh, cry, or even make you angry, but it is only the intention to finally be able to lay my burdens down...Are you ready for my truth?

I am going to share some text messages, screenshots from my phone to show you why I even decided to write this book. My hurt, my anger and the disrespect I received at the hands of my own siblings led me to want to speak my peace. The truth is, as complicated as our relationships are, I love them dearly and I have had to learn to love from a distance.

This text is from one of my sisters. My writing is on the right side of the screenshot. She consistently calls me a killer.

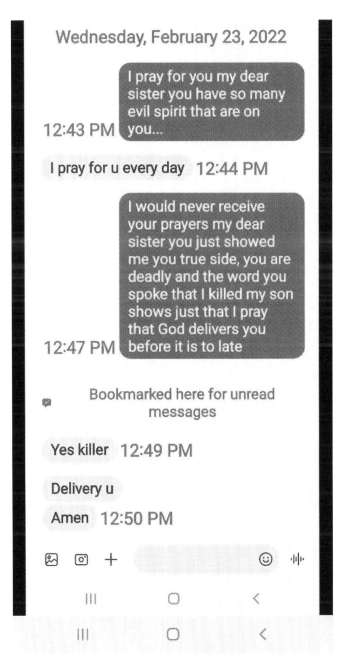

Wednesday, February 23, 2022

I pray for you my dear sister you have so many evil spirit that are on you... 12:43 PM

I pray for u every day 12:44 PM

I would never receive your prayers my dear sister you just showed me you true side, you are deadly and the word you spoke that I killed my son shows just that I pray that God delivers you before it is to late 12:47 PM

Bookmarked here for unread messages

Yes killer 12:49 PM

Delivery u

Amen 12:50 PM

You are very messy all you had to do was say u going this change and I would have understood i pray u find you way every where you go u cause trouble u better never say nothing else to me you take 30.000 dollars and blame everybody else of being a thief 9:10 AM

9:25 AM Ok lies and words yall say about can't hurt me. I LOVE YOU

I can't help u wanna hurt everybody cause u lost your son and his kids I pray u fine you way make a kid draw a punishment just to lie on there mother u r sick 9:27 AM

U didn't even have the respect to tell me that when u call u going to ache every day of your

My brother was being paid to care for my mother and father but had not done so. He would clock in while sitting in front of the house but would never go in to check on them. I went in to see about them when I came back to town and my mother had Covid-19 and was immediately hospitalized and placed on a ventilator. He was angry because he was no longer going to receive money to care for his parents, which he should have done for free.

U didn't even have the respect to tell me that when u call u going to ache every day of your life 9:30 AM

Ok   be careful the words you speak your child will be next 9:30 AM

You do your own sister bad well I pray u find your way Kathy dogg the shot out of you and you say nothing

This is the beginning of whats in store for you 9:32 AM

Let's show Facebook what my big brother is saying to me 9:34 AM

Go head and do that they will know u stole 30.000 thousands dollars from your dad to 9:35 AM

whats in store for you   9:32 AM

Let's show Facebook what my big brother is saying to me
9:34 AM

Go head and do that they will know u stole 30.000 thousands dollars from your dad to   9:35 AM

And I will.blass u like u never been.blass do it

I wish u would   9:36 AM

I don't care about that lie I'm about about to blast you and bug
9:36 AM

Do cause u got a lot to tell Facebook to   9:37 AM

9:37 AM   Let's go

Do it you will wish u never did   9:38 AM

After my mom and dad got out of the hospital, one of my brothers claimed that me and another sister made a list not allowing him to come to the hospital. No list existed, he just chose not to visit them. Once my parents were home, my brother walked into the front door after my parents were with the physical therapist and occupational therapist and was threatening everyone and the women called the police. I told him I would "Marvin Gaye" him if he continued the behavior. This is the result of that confrontation.

Wednesday, January 27, 2021

U don't wanna go to jail for murder u ever threatened me ur ass a be going to jail for lying in a murder investigation ! 1:33 PM

Read What fool

Read 1:43 PM You need help you bipolar ass fool

Read 1:45 PM Now go get yo ass some teeth that don't move NUT🤣

Uu killed ur df a on u fuckkn dummy by giving his crazy assortment ur keys u black ape 1:48 PM

U u killed uf son by giving his out of control ass ur keys ur black ape ! 1:49 PM

Read Stay off the drugs

keys ur black ape !   1:49 PM

Read Stay off the drugs
1:49 PM brother... lol

The truth hurts don't it
Blackwell!   1:50 PM

Read It's not helping you
Read You need help
1:50 PM

U should've told ur son
that maybe he wouldn't
went through a red light !   1:51 PM

U need help Blackwell
dtesling 40 thousand
dollars from ur own
father Blackie!   1:52 PM

U need help stealing 49
thousand dollars from ur
own father !   1:53 PM

Read Drugs and preacher don't
go together

Read Get help
1:54 PM

Read Oh I forgot nobody
acknowledges you as a
1:55 PM preacher...

lying never helps to get
insurance money for
the death of ur son u
dummy !
1:55 PM

Thats funny Gods does
but I guess everybody
scared to acknowledge
u as a murderer now go
figure Blackie!
1:57 PM

U funny but u can make
a baby with ur cousin
hahaha
2:01 PM

Bye you big mad mad
that you mad every
hate you.....INCLUDING
Read YOUR OWN KIDS NOW
2:02 PM GOODBYE

Chapter 1: The Love Story that Started it All

1 Corinthians 13 4-8

Love is patient, love is kind. It does not envy, it does not boast, it is not proud. It does not dishonor others, it is not self-seeking, it is not easily angered, it keeps no record of wrongs. Love does not delight in evil but rejoices with the truth. It always protects, always trusts, always hopes, always perseveres. Love never fails.

My parents originally met in the small town of Ringgold, Louisiana. When they got married my mom was 19 and my Daddy was 25. My parents are still together and will celebrate 63 years of marriage this year. Their courtship was short and they married in Kansas City, Missouri. Suspicion rocked their small town because people wondered whether my mom was already pregnant with my older sister. My family loves a good scandal, but I genuinely believe that their love for one another was the driving force that led my Daddy to run away from the comfort of his hometown to Kansas City where he would start his family and leave his legacy. Over the years I would tease my mom about the math of my oldest sister's birth and she finally admitted to me recently that she was in fact pregnant before they got married. It only took forever! I would classify my parent's relationship as a "beautiful nightmare." They have the type of love that you never want to wake up from, the type you never want to lose. Let me be clear, I did not say that their love came with no faults or mistakes. Their love is beautiful because they have had flaws, but their love is also favored. My parent's love story would be classified as something that is "perfectly imperfect". My Daddy was called to preach early on, and that love and respect that my mother had for my Daddy prepared him to accept his calling with no questions. Her love nurtured and prepared him for his calling. There was a reciprocation of love between them. My Daddy shared the same enthusiasm as my mother and took very seriously that God chose her to be his helpmate. Speaking from an honest place, I cannot say with certainty that she would not have chosen a different life if she had been given an alternative. However, my mom as they would say definitely "understood the assignment". Being called by God is not a task that should be taken lightly.

My Daddy had to be groomed and molded into a man of God, but my mom had to quickly adapt to being a first lady and all the many church hats that came with it. It is with utmost certainty that I can say that my mom was dedicated to her position as a first lady. In all actuality, my mother took all her roles very seriously. She made being a wife, mother, and first lady look effortless. While my mother managed her position with grace, her position burdened her just as heavily as it did my Daddy. For the sake of transparency, I will be upfront and share that my father ran from his calling in the beginning. He attempted to live in a way that the world considered to be "pleasurable". Luckily, my father stuck out like a sore thumb. My father had to realize, as Donald Lawrence would say, that he was, "not a natural being living a spiritual experience, but a spiritual being living a natural experience." Though my father found his calling, he did not escape his past life unscathed. My father would also agree with me that his past brought challenges to our family that left lasting effects on our family, and unknowingly to the generations that were to come. I have had many conversations with my father about his past, and it is interesting to visualize the metamorphosis that my Daddy had to go through to prepare for his calling as a man of God.

I do not want it to be misconstrued that I am judging my father because I am also one of those flawed and favored people that I spoke of earlier. I speak of these things not to place blame or create shame, but I speak of these things to promote growth and healing. It is because I know my Daddy's true character that I can grant him the same grace that the Lord grants to each one of us. We are created in the image of our father, but the duality of man is particularly important to understand why we sometimes fall prey to our fleshly desires. I cannot categorize my father's decisions as right or wrong. However, I can attest that it brought challenges to our family that impacted our lives. I am not here to put my father's life on trial, but I am here to show that our decisions can have lasting effects on the people that we love. For example, my oldest brother, who is the product of another relationship, has been one who can understand this all too well. He looks more like my Daddy than any of his sons but has had to come to terms with his identity. My father had his sister raise him as her own, which may seem common but there is much more to the story.

My father's sister presumably faked a pregnancy to convince her husband that the child belonged to her. My father reluctantly went along with the dramatic plot but vowed that he would never deny him if he were ever confronted with the truth. For 18 years my parent's love produced eight children thereafter, and years would pass before this secret would rear its ugly head and explode like a nuclear bomb. I always ask myself how my father thought that the secret would never be exposed with so many people knowing the truth? A dead giveaway was that my father openly supported him financially. He did so, not out of obligation but because he felt it was the right thing to do knowing that he was his biological son. There were other ways that my father made his position more pronounced, but nevertheless no one ever raised an eyebrow until direct confrontation ensued.

Coincidentally, the calamity would ensue during a Sunday morning church service. I can remember the moment so vividly that it is as if I am reliving the moment all over again every time I think of this experience. My Daddy was in the pulpit doing what he does best, and you could just tell that the spirit was moving at an all-time high. The entire church found themselves up on their feet singing praises and worshiping God. Getting the holy spirit moving through the church was what some people would call my father's "niche". My Daddy had a way of moving people with his words. When my Daddy found himself in the pulpit, you could just feel the connection that he had with God. It seemed as if everyone else in the audience felt the connection as much as my Daddy did. However, I cannot help but wonder about all the emotions and feelings that my nephew experienced in the moments before finding out the truth about his true ancestral ties to our family. My nephew said not only did his heart stop but so did time. The truth had my nephew so lost and confused that he had to remember to breathe. The shit figuratively hit the church ladies' fans. Confusion and pain consumed him. I can remember times that my nephew was kept away from us. We were robbed of time with my nephew and brother.

On the Sunday that this story unfolded, my nephew came to me and told me that another cousin, who was being messy, asked him, "how does it feel seeing your grandfather up there preachin' like this?" When my nephew, who is only a few years younger than me, walked into Daddy's office after church he asked him, with tears in his eyes, "are you my grandfather?" Daddy told him that he would never deny them if ever they asked and so he responded with a resounding yes. They embraced and Daddy explained everything. It was a tough moment and there were so many things that were answered, like why he always received money from his uncle in college. I have these feelings that I bear. You see, I carry the name Geneva. This name is my aunt's name that hid this secret and pretended to be the real mother of my brother. She was actually his aunt. She died in 1975 and I was born in 1976 and named to honor her. For years I hated the name because I believed she stole my father's baby. When I hear that name I bear the sorrow for my Daddy. I bear the secrets. He is always trying to make up for what he didn't get to do for my brother. My brother actually thought that he was an incest baby between Daddy and Aunt Geneva when in reality she faked a pregnancy.

When my nephew went to meet his real grandmother she didn't deny him he just said, "I don't know what you are talking about son…" The mother, the real mother, as a young woman became pregnant by Daddy. The young woman threatened to give their baby away if Daddy did not marry her. He wasn't in love with her at all so he refused to marry her. Instead of giving the baby away, Aunt Geneva stepped in. She wasn't able to get pregnant by her second husband so she took the baby. After about a year and a half the woman came back for her baby but my aunt, who was really a bully, ran the young girl away by threatening her. My brother, who was raised as my cousin, was never close to us. This is where the lies and the secrets get passed down and disrupt the lives and identities of people who don't even have a choice in the matter.

Going back to my father, just like his connection to God, my interconnectedness to my father is almost unimaginable. My Daddy has always been my saving grace, and anyone who knows me can attest that I am the true definition of a "Daddy's girl". I adored the fact that my Daddy loved God more than anything. My father's beginnings and transgressions were meant to happen. God used my Daddy's faults to break him down to his simplest form. The Lord did this to allow my Daddy to be used to the fullest of capacities. Had my father been without stains, arrogance might have set in. My Daddy sacrificed everything to show his love for God. He sacrificed himself, his integrity, his wife, and even his children.

There were many days and nights that I watched him break down and cry from the lack that he felt. My Daddy mourned his brokenness in silence because only the One who called him could restore him. Accepting his calling was a very heavy burden that may have been too great for some to understand. For some reason, I was always the one who understood him and saw him for who he truly was. The connection that we have could surely withstand the tests of time, and for that I will always love and protect him.

You are probably wondering *where is the love in all of this*? As of now, it seems as if my mom was the only one making sacrifices and loving in my parent's marriage. However, I urge you to remove your own thoughts and biases to allow you to see things from a unique perspective. When I talk about the love story that started it all, I am not referring to my parent's love story. Their love was just a product of the real "love story" that I was referring to. You see, let me explain. The greatest love cannot be between people. People live in the world and are of flesh which produces love that sometimes comes with many conditions. The greatest love is spiritual that allows for true supernatural submission. My father was given an order from God, and with it came hard sacrifices and decisions that may not be understood by the world. It is because my father loved God that he had to begin to turn away from his worldly desires. I can see these things about my father and my family because of my unique position. I have siblings who are old enough to be my parents so my nieces and nephews are like siblings to me because of their ages. You can say that this position really straddles me between worlds because although I am a sibling, I have often been treated as a child and my nieces and nephews have confided in me as a friend, not as an aunt. This enmeshment has allowed me to really see life differently, to be able to understand what makes us all human and holy.

Had you paid attention, I said that my mom was also groomed for her position as a first lady. The vessel of whom God chose to use for my earthly experience was a battle that proved to be one of the biggest hurdles in my life. The children of whom my mom would birth would be the brokenness of her that would come to fruition. Her sorrows, her lack, and her insecurities would surface in the present in the faces of each and one my siblings, including myself. You see, the position that was chosen and accepted by my mother left her with many decisions. I do not want you to think that I have negative feelings towards my mother. I love her with all my heart, and would do anything for her. It is completely understandable that my mother made a few mistakes.

You see, my mother was a great first lady. I will not take that away from her! However, in any leadership position it can be difficult to just live your life. It seems as if you are always in the spotlight. People are always watching you, and with my mother it was no different. Growing up, it almost seemed that my mom could only be herself inside the parameters of our four walls. There were no expectations, and my mom could just simply be. My mom just had a way of speaking life into her children. When my mother would tell us we could do something, it would always come true. I remember her telling my brother and sister that they would be teach many. She told my brother that he had a musical gift and he found himself being the minister of music. Most importantly, she told me that I would be a nurse and it came to fruition. She saw something in each of us, and it would always come to life. I just can't help but wish that my mom had given herself the same motivational speeches. My mom was a virtuous woman, and though she had her struggles, I can say that some of my best qualities have come from her. There were moments that I found my mother's actions to be astonishing. One thing that I have to remember is that behavior is learned, and I can say with utmost certainty that my mother fell victim, just like us, to those same unhealthy teachings. The display of toxic behavior came from ancestors too. All the generational curses and hurt clearly manifested in her decisions. Her calling was to do better for the generation that she birthed. She did a better job of this than those who came before her...well at least that is how she made it seem. I am here to place no judgment, but I will say that my mother taught me how to be an Emmy award winning actor when I needed to be. I do not want you to confuse being anointed with being perfect. She made some mistakes, but she held more power than what she believed. At times, my mother selfishly moved which made room for others around her to suffer the consequences. This may seem harsh, but I have left room for explanation to allow my mother to heal and share her truth when she feels so obligated to do so. I have not always been in this place but I think when I finally stepped outside of myself as a daughter and just looked at my mom as a woman I can see how complicated her life really was. And Mommy, if you are reading this I want you to know that you are a phenomenal woman!

Who better to tell the story of us than me. I was born March 19, 1976 in Kansas City, Missouri to Mary Louise Rambo and Pastor Julius Rambo. For the first time I will acknowledge I am the baby of **ten** (not nine) children and I will answer the question everyone wants to know: YES, I AM SPOILED! I got every single thing I ever wanted. If I asked for it I got it. I don't remember having a bad childhood. It just was, if I asked, I received. Jordans, games, a car. I got my first car right after I graduated high school. My Dad bought me a two-seater sports car and I drove it until the wheels fell off, literally, while on my way to a hair appointment. I was never a kid who had to have everything, they always beat me to ask for what I wanted. My parents anticipated what I wanted. What my parents didn't provide me with, my Godmother gave to me. But there were things I did need that my parents could not give me and that was the conversation of how to be, how to live life as a teenager in that day and time. I just remember my parents were always older than everyone else's parents. Hilarious enough, my mom and my sister were pregnant at the same time. I always tell them that one of them shouldn't have been pregnant and I will let them decide who that might be. My parents tried raising my siblings and I using the same parenting style. When I look back I see it wasn't wrong, it just needed some minor adjustments. I took the same style with my son but I tweaked it a little. I tweaked it a little more with my granddaughters. You see, my parents had children that were 20 years apart so when my oldest sister had to be home by 10 pm for homecoming, during my time the party was just getting started. It is fine being raised with the same morals and values but the practice of those values have to look different to change with the times.

This book is all about permission, give yourself the permission to tell your story, your truth. As long as I have breath, my mouth will never close to the truth. I am very opinionated, will always express my feelings and my mom will say, "baby, sometimes you have to let God fight your battles," and I would respond with, "well God gave us a mouth to use. We cannot let those who misuse us get away with everything. Sometimes you have to speak out..." she will nod in agreement and say, "for that, baby girl, I thank you."

Chapter 2: The Church

Church was instilled in me from an incredibly early age. So much so, I joke that my first words were "God" and "hallelujah". It was not just my immediate family though. The thirst for God stretched deep into my family's Southern roots. My family is full of pastors, musicians, and vocalists. The Rambo name rings so many bells in the ears of people in my city. We are known as a major contributor to the church world. Speaking for myself, I have acted in every play, sang in every choir, and did every role in the church that could be entrenched in my Baptist upbringing except for pastor. Church was the norm for me, and I loved every minute of it. I am well versed in the church, which means I have seen it all. I have seen the good, the bad, and even the things in between. I had witnessed many things that I was almost unconsciously groomed to ignore. My issue was that I could never just ignore the things I had issues with. I could never just "keep quiet" because God gave me my voice, and I felt that I was obligated to use it. Who was I to not utilize the gift God had given me? Throughout all the changes in church, one thing that remained constant throughout all the "church chaos" was my father. Like previously stated, I will tell you that I have always thought my father was a phenomenal man. He had a way to make you awestruck with his words. Daddy just had a way about him that would draw people to him. Graceful and respectful would be just a few words that I would use to describe him as a leader. One thing that would blow my mind would be how he never took credit for what God placed in his heart to speak to people.

You know, I have always had a calling on my life, well, an anointing if you will. I remember at the meager age of seven going up to a woman named Sister Smith and asking, "Do you like this church?" When she responded yes, something just came over me and with the utmost confidence I told her, "You should join then!" The spirit in me always drew people to me in a way that I am just now beginning to understand. Again, I am just another anecdote to show how you have to be groomed for your destiny. I know that my gift was placed upon me by God, and even when I went astray, I was always one of God's biggest cheerleaders. I always wanted people to experience the love of God that I had. You could always find me trying to lead people to the God who had saved a wretch like me. No matter the circumstances, God is and always will be first in my life. What I have experienced firsthand is that God will test you. In James 1:12 it reminds us that, "*blessed is the man who remains steadfast under trial, for when he has stood the test, he will receive the crown of life.*" God has tested me numerous times, and the tests have changed my ideology about what I should let into my life. The idea that I once had of church has completely morphed. My spiritual journey has led me to find out that things I put much stock into are the main things that I no longer subscribe to. It is mind-boggling to think that I may have placed man on a pedestal that I now know that they were not deserving of. It was not until I truly established my own relationship with God that I was able to decipher between those who say they are called, and those who truly are. This brings to mind Psalms 118 that says, "*It is better to take refuge in the Lord than to trust man.*" I have seen leaders of the church speak and preach one thing but live another. Not all, but many people labeled as saints live prideful and selfish lives. The word clearly states that pride is not of the father but is of the world. Simply put, I have seen every commandment of the bible be broken by the ones who say they were called into the fold of the Lord.

Now, I get that man is flawed but it is scary to think that these are the people who are supposed to be the catalysts of healing the broken. Their duty is to draw people near God, not just in word but also by actions. Personally, I am deeply saddened by the actions of the church and I feel that issues need to be publicly addressed. We have to speak publicly against the things that are wrong in the sight of God. I have witnessed pastors ridicule people when they should be uplifting them. Come on people of God, when will we stand up? Bringing it closer to home, I went through the most traumatic, life altering event that is any mother's worst nightmare. I cannot say that I felt supported by the church, and for the sake of transparency I would say that it felt as if they turned their backs on me. It seemed as if I got pain when I needed peace. I got accused when I needed assurance, and most importantly I got silence when I needed to be surrounded. It is hard to believe that all this happened at the hands of the church. I am still in disbelief over the events that took place when my only child passed away in a car accident. The things that were said to me, the actions I saw from people, and most crucially all the hurt it caused are still symptoms that I work through to this very day.

I want to also discuss this idea of correction in the church when it comes to leadership. Sometimes church leaders want to correct others for all the wrong reasons. Leaders need to make sure their correction isn't because they are offended by someone's personality and that they should not hinder anyone's walk with Christ. Oftentimes I find leaders use this word, "correction" as a license to control and manipulate God's people. When one is in leadership they should be open to correction themselves. Of course this should be done in private but correction must be done nonetheless. They should also learn to admit when they are wrong as opposed to hiding behind these false religious walls called, "Touch Not My Anointed".

Leadership should be transparent, humble, and have a servant's heart. Too many leaders believe their own press and hold themselves in higher esteem than God. They feel like they are above reproach and that anyone who hasn't "accomplished" what they think they have accomplished, that person doesn't have the "authority" to "correct" them. And yet scripture contradicts such heresy. Paul commended the Berean Church for searching out the scriptures themselves to ensure what he was sharing was actually the word of God.

Jesus commended the Church of Ephesus for "rebuking" those who claimed to be Apostle but were not. Too many of these leaders want to "correct" people. Very few of you want to take the time to "pray" for them (and pray prayers by the SPIRIT and NOT out of the dictates of your own heart and flesh). Leadership is a slippery slope, hence the reason why Paul said not many should seek the position, without fully understanding the cost. The sheep are NOT yours - they believe in God. It would behoove us to remember that. "He suffered no man to do them wrong: yea, he reproved kings for their sakes; Saying, Touch not mine anointed, and do my prophets no harm."
- Psalms 105:14, 15

Notice who God actually spoke to when he said, "Touch not my anointed" It wasn't His people. It was the LEADERSHIP He instructed NOT to touch his anointed (his sheep, his people). I believe we need to start teaching THIS instead of focusing on "correcting" God's people. As leaders we need to correct ourselves! Too many of us are "touching God's anointed..."

I have seen pastors use social media to entice women without showing pictures of their wives on any parts of their profiles. It is clear that they are using their power to draw the attention of women not in the church. Another pastor talked about people using social media to gain attention and then he turned around the very next day stating all of these horrible statements to people who are having funerals in a slew of posts. NO ONE CORRECTED EITHER OF THESE MEN! I know that may be hard for many to hear not only when it comes to leadership but also because I am a woman saying these things.

I have not given up on the church because I know that the Lord has a plan that will eventually come to fruition but I have definitely been church hurt. One day the church will do and be what God intended. Until then, it will take the efforts of the entire fold to restore the brokenness of the church. The church is a body of Christ, a body of Christ that is formed by the bodies of the people. We can no longer allow the church to portray this idea that man should be followed. It is imperative that we return to God what belongs to him. The thing about our Father is that he allows us the freedom of choice...even when our choices are not of God. My hope is that the church will not have to fall completely before it realizes that changes need to be made. Are we willing to allow the people to fail because of selfish pride? I am not sure who this is meant for, but I want to let you know that you can be used by God. Do not let the world around you tell you otherwise. Show up, and be willing to let God in, and who knows the lives you could touch. He saved me and he can save you too.

Chapter 3: The Final Straw

I will say before I begin this chapter that this will probably be very difficult for some to read. Honestly, writing this book has been a challenge within itself, but reliving the days and moments surrounding my son's death has been so difficult. I ask that you go with me on this journey and remain prayerful throughout this heart-wrenching experience. Now, let us begin! I remember the day so vividly; I was lying in my sister's bed when I got the call. I was home at the time to be with my sister because her husband of 31 years passed away from cancer. Losing my brother was a huge loss for the family due to him and my sister being together since I was a little girl. To know one of them was to know the other. All I knew is that my sister needed me and so my son loaded up the car and we headed to KC. I was so sad for my sister because she couldn't bear life without her husband. She was so grief stricken. "Can you stay a little longer, Eva?" I heard my big sister pleading with me in all of her grief, and all I could do was agree.

One day turned into two, and then turned into three, and so forth. I knew eventually that I would have to go back to Nashville, but I knew that right now Kansas City was where I needed to be. I would have to leave and return to my own life, but before that we needed to have a wang, dang, doodle. One thing about my family is that we know how to throw a great party. We had a kickback the night before, and we were up until 4:00 am. It was so much fun but something was peculiar about that night. The funny thing is that I was not the only one who thought so. We played games, sang songs, and just used the opportunity to enjoy our family… My son, who is always on ten thousand, was super chill that night. So much so my sister asked him, "Dude, are you high?" He looked up to her and said, "No auntie, I ain't high, I am just chilling." It was such a good time! I was singing to him while grabbing his face and he did not resist at all. He allowed me to have fun with him as he usually does, but before we called it a night, Robert begged to use my car. For whatever reason, I agreed and gave him my keys, and he promised to have it back early in the morning as he left the party. I normally wouldn't have let him take the car but this time I did. Although we stayed up to the wee hours of the morning, I was still somewhat awake when Robert called me at 10:00 am.

"Momma, I am on my way to bring the car."

"I am still in bed son, just wait until noon."

Then we disconnected.

As I laid around, the mother of one of Robert's children kept calling me. I refused to answer because she and Robert had been at odds with each other, and I wanted no involvement in their mess. Ten minutes later, I got a call from his Daddy at approximately 11:45am.

He said, "Eva, is little Robert with you?"

I asked, "Why?"

He then said, "There is a really bad car accident near my house." His voice trailed off as I hopped out the bed. I heard him say, "They are saying the car looks exactly like yours with out of state tags." He began to inform me that he was on his way there and would call me back after he found out more information…I said to him, frantically "Hell naw! You can't go see shit for me, I got to go check on my baby for myself." My sister was outside and was talking to our brother as I began to race to the car. I was in sheer panic mode and it prompted my sister to ask me what was wrong.

I told her that I felt something was wrong with my baby. She started to plead the blood of Jesus as I felt myself go numb. My son's baby mother called back and she asked, "Ms. Geneva, is Robert in your car?" I responded saying yes. She said, "It's a wreck up here and the person is dead, but I can't get too close." She elaborated and let me know that the car did not look like mine. For some reason, this did not bring me comfort and I yelled to my sister to take me to the scene of the accident. At the time, she was on the phone with my brother explaining what we were hearing. All while she was driving, she was hyperventilating and in a full blown panic attack. I can truly say that it was nothing but God that we got there safely. I cried all the way there saying, "Oh God, Oh Jesus," repeatedly while rubbing my hands and rocking back and forth.

There was a chill that came over me when we arrived. When we arrived on the scene, Robert was there but I couldn't get close enough to the actual accident. We quickly veered off to the side to allow a path to the car. Everyone else in my family took off running like track stars to get closer. I was in a daze, walking in a drunk stupor. They were met by the police and I could see my sister and Robert's dad drop to the ground as if they didn't have bones while the police spoke with plain faces. I never made it to where his body was because I had lost all control and fell to the ground. I remember coming to and having to call my significant other to let him know about the tragedy that had occurred. It was like his mind couldn't process or compute what I was saying. He wanted to cry but it was as if his mind would not let him process the thought. I just kept saying, "My baby is gone! My baby is gone!" He just couldn't wrap his head around it. He asked, "What happened, did someone shoot him?"

I quickly said, "No, he was in a car wreck." Even saying it didn't feel right, and I couldn't believe it was coming out of my mouth. I wasn't ready to accept it. He always was so good about asking what I needed him to get for me, or what I wanted him to do for me. I can say that even in this trying time he didn't fail to make sure that I was doing okay given the circumstances. It was hard telling him, but it made it start to become real.

I was so saddened by the thought that my baby died alone. He needed me for everything and I was always there for him. I could not fathom that I was not there with my baby when he transitioned. He was there without me and it made me wonder, *"Was he alone? Did he cry out for me?"* My mind instantly thought about the effect that this would have on my grandbabies. He left four beautiful baby girls and two bonus daughters behind. I couldn't make it make sense in my head at that moment and even sometimes now. I often wonder, *"why, just why?"* The news traveled so fast...almost faster than the speed of light. At this point, another brother pulled up and fell out almost instantaneously. The whole scene was gut-wrenching to watch, but the only thing I could think about was that the only child I ever had was gone.

My only child, who was only twenty-six, was gone seemed to be the only words that came to mind. What was I supposed to do without my baby? The accident happened three blocks from his Daddy's house and his paternal grandfather saw the wreck after Robert sped past him. He went home and told his son he had just seen a horrible wreck. There were so many accounts about what happened at the scene. Things like, Robert ran a red light, he was being chased by the police, and so many outrageous tales. You would not believe that some of those lies came from family members, even one that I allowed to speak at my son's funeral. It is true that he was speeding, but contrary to popular belief he did not run a red light. Others involved did have injuries, but my son was the only fatality.

Everything was a blur for me at this point, and it was almost as if I blocked it out like it didn't happen. I was in denial. Some would say that I was in complete and utter disbelief.

Another brother pulled up and instantly said, "We need to get her away from here!" I told him, "I can't leave my baby here." It felt like he was being selfish. What he did not realize was that he gets to go home with his child and I would have to leave my baby in the street. At the moment, all I was looking for was a little sensitivity but my brother did not seem to understand. After all of the formalities, I was taken away from the scene of the accident and taken back to my sister's house. Back at the house, my brother gave a whole damn speech about us needing to come together so that we can pull some things together to pay for his funeral. I was so insulted! How dare he think that I had not made the correct provisions for my only child in the case of his death? I was dying inside, but the insults were so overwhelming that they could not be ignored. I was more than pissed! The conversations going on around me while I am literally dying on the inside were horrible.

My brother's wife thought she had the authority to say who got to stay and who had to leave. She insisted that my cousin had to leave. My cousin said that she would not leave and she stood her ground. Everything was about them, but right at that moment my son was laying in the middle of the street, lifeless. I was the one who was hurting, not them, and how could they not see this? The shenanigans that took place made it clear to me that my siblings did not care about me or my son. I could not help but think to myself, *Why would you leave me Robert, you know I cannot be ok without you?* My cousin called our shared doctor because she saw me crashing and knew I would need medical intervention. My doctor called back and my cousin let her know that I was not okay. Not only did they keep trying to make my cousin leave, but they also kept insisting I did not have any insurance on my baby. Why the hell is that so fucking important while I'm sitting here dealing with the biggest tragedy of my life? I was literally living every mother's worst nightmare. I recall hearing whispers that said, "She needs to go to a place where nobody can get to her..." My brother's wife of course assigned herself as the overseer saying, "I will not let anybody over here." I understood what she was trying to do but I was not going to go along with their plan. The sad truth is that she did not care for my son or for me, and her previous actions in his life as well as those after his death showed this. My son and I were loved by so many people, but I knew deep down that she was not one of them. *"You are thinking selfishly. I can fend for myself."* I thought.

At this point, my sister had taken my phone and began telling everyone that I could not talk. Like I said before, I understood what they were trying to do but they were telling this to people that I felt like I needed to talk to. The people they were turning away were the people who when my siblings misused and abused me were always present for me. I wanted to intervene and request that my niece handle everything because I knew she had my best interest at heart. However, I was just too weakened to say this at the time. The next place that I found myself at was my godmother's house. One thing that I knew for sure was that she was going to take care of me, like she always had. I was placed in a bed and I could not take phone calls. Talk about deja vu. I managed to get the phone and it seemed as if I was a child all over again. I quickly called my niece and asked her to come get me. I wanted my phone because I needed to see my son's face. I shared that,"I have to go. I need to leave," and made my way to my niece's house.

Sadly, I don't think anyone thought about his Daddy, his wife, or my significant other. We all lost a son. We all were affected in a way that would change us forever. Our mates were instrumental in our son's upbringing. I recall one day that Robert's Daddy called and he had just cried on the phone for so long. He finds himself frequently going to places where he and Robert would go to just sit and cry. No one knows the real impact of the pain that he lives with everyday. He goes to work, and works long hours but he is not okay. He tells me often, "I don't know what to do..." I understood this feeling all too well because when people would call me to ask the simple question of how are you feeling, I would find myself breaking down. They would tell me not to cry, not knowing that this is the worst thing to say. I knew deep down that they meant well, but my son would never come back. He would never be able to tuck his girls in, or tell me happy Mother's Day, and so it was heartbreaking to hear the words, "don't cry" when crying was all that I wanted to do.

Grief is such a personal thing and you just have to go through it to understand it. I now realize why people throw birthday parties five years after the death of a loved one, or post their pictures continuously, or go to their grave a lot. Before, I was guilty of thinking people were taking too long to heal. I now have to apologize for that short-sighted thinking because now I get it, I truly get it. The pain comes in waves; Sometimes they are like a tsunami, but other times it comes with a slight ripple. Under the circumstances, I did not think that after the accident that I could be any more traumatized. Well, news flash, I had thought wrong! I had a lot of anxiety with the funeral planning, but I didn't want anyone else to do it. My son and I talked about what we both wanted in the past and I wanted to make sure his wishes were carried out, even in the midst of a pandemic. I wanted to be sure to give him the funeral that he deserved. When going to meet with the funeral home, I remember just thinking I needed to get everything in place that he wanted to have. Even the pallbearers mattered to him, and I wanted to make sure all those things were in place.

Jumping back in time, I can remember when we went to sign the insurance policy when he was about nineteen years old. He was very uncomfortable with signing the insurance policy. Of course, we had never thought that it would be me collecting money on his behalf. It is not an easy conversation to have but all families need to do it. I had already been through so much seeing him laying in the street, but dealing with the funeral home was a next level struggle. You see, they never asked me for an insurance policy, and ended up incorrectly assuming that the policy was through my job. I got a phone call that my insurance policy was not active, and I quickly told him that the policy comes out of my account monthly. The funeral home claimed to have called, but the number they gave me was incorrect. I proceeded to call my insurance agency. This funeral home put a rush on the death certificate and that would cost $1500. I experienced the business of the funeral home. I paid $7000 for my son's funeral but my sister's family had to pay $13,000 for the exact same service. It is an ugly business. The popular funeral home took liberties and assumptions they should not have. To this day, they have not returned money that is due to me. Again, I felt as if my fragile mental state had been taken advantage of. On the other hand, my insurance agent took care of me and protected me.

I don't know if there were different guidelines but I was told that we couldn't have family cars, but I saw other funeral homes had family cars. I felt like there were things about my son's funeral that he was robbed of. I went with the popular funeral home, and now looking back I felt I should have gone with another funeral home. After dealing with the funeral home, the pandemic made things even worse. We found out that due to government regulations, both sides of the family were to get only forty-five people. The problem with this was that our families are huge. It was an uphill battle to select such a minuscule amount of people. Nevertheless, I made my list and his Daddy's family made their list. The upsetting part was that my brother and his wife maliciously played the role of club bouncers by letting people they wanted in and removed those from the list they didn't want. His wife used that moment as a point of attack on people she didn't like. Even though both of them had proven to me so many other times that they were incapable of being a pastor and first lady, I had thought they would have had a change of heart. I told myself surely this situation will be different but it was not. People like my mom's siblings and Daddy's siblings weren't allowed in, but her friends were allowed in to view my son's body. To make matters worse, they were able to stay for the funeral while family was denied. I was so furious! My sister-in-law had shown her true colors and used my son's death to further her own selfish, evil agenda. I had taken the hurt and disrespect from my family for years, but after my son passed I knew that enough was enough!

After Robert left this earth, one of my first thoughts went to my grandbabies. I guess Beyonce said it best when she said, "I want my unborn son to be like my Daddy." I didn't know how much of this dream I spoke into a reality at the time. My son could not create a boy if his life depended on it. The connection that he had with his children was one of the best I had ever witnessed. I can still remember how I found out about my very first grandbaby.

It was a Tuesday night, when I got the call from my son and his first child's mother. Robert called me through messenger, and was just staring me in my face. He finally introduced us, and then told told she was having his baby. These two weren't ready for the cussing I was about to dish out. They stood firm and listened to every word I said.

I asked Robert, "Why the fuck would yo' dumb ass go out and get a damn baby."

I looked at her and said, "What the hell do you think ,you won a prize possession or something? This boy ain't got a pot to piss in nor a window to throw it out of."

I then told Robert, "I hope yo' stupid ass know to get a blood test." Diamond finally broke her silence and in the most humbled, but secure voice she said, "Ms. Geneva, you're more than welcome to have a blood test done."I talked to her so crazy that I have to say that I respected her for being able to stand up to me. The two of them did not have an official relationship, but I know that they had a special love for one another. We have grown so close with one another that I treat her as my own.

I met the other mother of his children on a birthday cruise. She was definitely a pecuLIAR little lady, but because my son loved her, I loved her. It was almost as if she was fighting for a position that she already had. We have come to an understanding with one another that because of how she felt about my son that I would always love her. I went through things with both of them, but one thing for sure is that I will always love my grandbabies. I will do anything for those girls because that is what my son would have wanted. The girls love their Daddy, and will always remember him as being present and loving. I will never forget June 3, 2016, March 6, 2017, or March 12, 2018 (twins) because those are the days that my grandbabies blessed the world with their presence. Every time I look at my grandbabies I see my son, and for that I will forever have love for their mothers.

After my baby passed, I knew I wanted to celebrate him by having a balloon release. Showing up to the balloon release would make it real that my baby was gone. Me being me, I had to have an edible or two to make it through the event. When I arrived, my high was broken when I saw how many lives my son touched. They all showed up for him because he was truly loved. Here is an account from a friend, Paris London, who witnessed his last moments of life. I have permission to share this facebook post:

> *Poor baby, I saw the whole thing unfold, from when you wrecked to when the coroner came to pick up your body. Damn dude, why tf were you going that fast? Why did you do this man? I know your goofy ass is looking down from heaven like look what my black ass did. These tears are turning to happy ones because you don't have to hurt any more. It is crazy because I am a very spiritual person, and I most definitely believe in the after life. Everyone at the scene kept asking is that Rob? Right before the coroner came to pick you up, the yellow tarp that covered your body flew up. I truly believe that you were letting everyone know to stop worrying. I am glad to have known you! It was a pleasure. Rest in heaven black ass!*

When I scrolled on Facebook and saw this message it gave me so much peace that he was not alone when he died. When I reached out to her again for permission to use the quote above, I found great comfort in her words. Even hearing from her again let me know he did not suffer at all. His death was not one of pain and that while we all hurt, he is ok. I also know that when my older sister left this earth, she would take care of my baby for me and that they were together. I am surprised what has brought me peace because there was a time that I never thought that I would get here.

I am left with sweet memories of him as my only child. Many people think only children are spoiled but even as a child Robert was just the opposite. He was a positive presence in people's lives. I am realizing now as I write this, that we mothers are chosen vessels, ordained by God, to give the best of who we are to our children. I realize the 26 years I was given with my son was a blessing. I think about how much of a giver he was. He was about 12 years old and there was a Caucasian girl that lived on our block and to look at her with the naked eye her clothes were always dingy and so was her face. He would come home and talk about this girl that everyone teased and it really bothered him. It was instilled in us to care for the injured bird. One day he thought it was a good idea to give this little girl a brand new pair of Jordans. I was livid that he gave the $150 pair of shoes to the little girl. God spoke directly to me and said not to punish him for this great deed. "Want for others what you want for yourself." Nothing material had value to him. If he had it, everyone else around him had it. I watched her go up and down the street with the tennis shoes on and she was so happy and had a new walk about herself.

Robert was also crafty and handy. When he was five I told him if you can't crack the crab then you can't eat them. He kept grabbing wire pliers and was determined to learn. "I need them so I can learn how to crack my own crabs". I even learned over time why Robert enjoyed marijuana and edibles. His death has suspended my own judgment about even small things I may have been upset about in the past.

Another gift that Robert left me is the gift of the mothers of his children. They are the Naomi to my Ruth. They carried my legacy and are raising my granddaughters beautifully. Diamond and LaTrice, both of you possess unique qualities I appreciate. You both have a position in my heart. He loved you in different ways and I love you both for your children. I will always pour into each of you, I hope you all will continue to grow and learn together; that we all remain tied and all love on each other. Let us continue to be the circle of love that is Robert. For those of you suffering great losses, know that with prayer and time, you will gain a new peace.

Chapter 4: The Family

Where do I start when it comes to my family? There is just so much that has transpired when it comes to my family. I will start by saying that it is not my ideology to slander or blame others. As I previously stated, this is my truth and I can only tell it how I experienced it to be. The bullshit does not start with my immediate family. Our toxicity stems from the very beginning of our bloodline. I will no longer be quiet and allow the shenanigans to continue. You may ask the questions, *who does she think she is*? *What gives her the right to speak of these things*? Well, the authority of which I tell these tales comes from the same God that this family has served my entire life. This family must heal, and for this to happen it must be exposed. My family has kept quiet about the rape, incest, manipulation, lies, and drug dependencies for far too long. To this I say no more! One sin begets another, and like lies, you cannot tell just one! Let us start with the most disturbing secret that I believe has done unmeasurable damage. Both sides of my family are huge and all of them migrated from the same town of Ringgold, Louisiana. As you know, Ringgold is small, and everyone is related in some way...or should we say connected in some way. The wandering mind may wonder if there is a tad bit of inbreeding going on. Let us talk about it! About my family, some were protected, and some were not. My siblings and I were not exposed to one side of my family. A reasonable person would ask the question why, and I will gladly explain to you the reason.

The reason is because some male family members were taking advantage of the female members. The hard truth is that female members experienced rape at the hands of their own blood. I am baffled as to why this was allowed. I say allowed because it was all kept secret, and it began to foster an environment that made the male members think that their behavior was acceptable. In the simplest of terms, grown ass men were having sex with the younger girls, and it was a known fact that was kept quiet. The fucked up part is that the young girls were condemned because of what the secrets drove them to do. This destroyed them, and to cope they had to use coping mechanisms that deemed them incapable of functioning normally.

Let us be real, if the root were dealt with it would have divulged the sinful nature of the figures who held so much weight in our family. What is more fucked up is that there were open discussions, everyone knew, but only some would take the necessary precautions so that it did not happen to their daughters. My heart goes out to the others who were not protected. Instead, my family protected the perpetrators, the rapists, the people who used their status to take advantage of young girls. You are probably wondering how my parents fit into all of this? Well, the truth is my mother was one of those victims. Hence, the reason she carried brokenness with her all her life. My Daddy wanted to avenge the victims, and for a quick second he forgot his calling and wanted to kill the villains. As a family we would watch shows and real life drama going through the exact same issues without dealing with the evilness in our own family. Until we deal with the evilness in our own family we have no right to even try to talk about what other families, real or imagined, should and shouldn't be doing when we are quiet in the name of Christian love and forgiveness. My family is very judgmental when it comes to other people so I want to remind us all, "Judge not, that ye be not judged." —Matthew 7:1

We all know that siblings bicker, well my family makes a boxing match look like a playdate. For example, one of my sisters, who has dependency and addiction issues for as long as I can remember, has accused me of murdering my own child yet she has the blood of her own children on her hands. The village raised her children, and they cannot comfortably speak the name momma because they have not experienced what that is. The beast that ultimately was the demise of one of her children was fed by her. The demons that chased her were transferred to her child and she was not able to fight the demon, which caused her to succumb to the fight. I almost feel like she believed it was the way to escape this bullshit.

My brother who has what appears to be the greatest calling of our siblings is a leader, but yet he does not lead. He allows his wife, who in my sight, does not put the greater good of God's people first. He worries about keeping her happy rather than her being his help and trusting the will of the One who provides all. She creates separation rather than unification when she has the power to create the environment of what she lacks. I saw firsthand who my brother was as a leader when he put my son out of his church not once, not twice, but three different times! All my son wanted to do was utilize the gift that God gave him. My son just wanted to play the drums, but my brother seemed to want to tear him down. The issue started because my son was playing drums for free. After a long time they were willing to pay another musician weekly that was less than consistent. Instead of dealing with the equality around pay, he fired my son (from a volunteer position) because he said he had a bad attitude.

The second issue involved growing the Praise and Worship Ministry. Robert was pulled back on the drums and agreed to do it for free for his godfather, who led the ministry. Once he rejoined he was then was told by the pastor (who was his uncle) that he could not play the drums. His wife was instrumental in getting my son fired AGAIN even after a person was given power to find his staff. I muscled though Praise and Worship that Wednesday (I was on the team) and after that I said, "Lord, release me," and I left to never return as a member.

The third time was my niece's funeral in which Robert wanted to play as a tribute for his cousin he deeply loved. Robert went to the rehearsal and the drummer that was there agreed Robert should play. My brothers told him again that he was not allowed to play. They went as far as to call the police on my son to make him leave the church. He even told him he couldn't attend the funeral. As a leader you should be bringing people into the church, not turning them away. My brother tried to take away my son's gift, and it makes me wonder what else he has taken? They really hurt my baby and he never shared with his uncles how much it knocked the spiritual wind out of him. When church is also family, it is a double blow. I did not want my brothers to preach and play over my son's body at his funeral because all of that hurt was never resolved. When I prayed about it I heard God say it should be so because although my brothers did my baby so wrong, they knew him best, they knew the pureness of his heart.

Another older sister, who was the standard in my eyes, was not who she told me she was. I looked up to her and wanted to be like her and as I started to progress the same love was not returned. She would be happy for you as long as you did not surpass her. My sister wanted the world to think she had everything, but all I saw from her was brokenness. Everything needed to be a competition for her, but for me I was just living my life. I did not need to compete because the brokenness was all the same. She would never let the world see the truth. My sister is the type that if she didn't post it, it didn't happen. She would only post things that would paint her in a positive light. I may have missed the post, but I wonder did she post about how her children profited off my son? It took some time, but God has taken the weariness out of my heart. I have forgiven her but I hope that the sister I once looked up to will one day return.

The gifted musician of the family is affected by opioid addiction and has been emotionally, verbally, and mentally abusive to his family. It is to the point that his wife accepts the emotional abuse because she once saw him as her saving grace. My brother is a boy masquerading as a man. This same man took part in putting my son out of the church. He had the audacity to cry and play the music over my son's body, but he hurt the woman Robert loved more than anyone, his mother, me. Is he a minister of music or a minister of malice?

All of my siblings weren't called to lead; some were just supposed to be. This brother couldn't resist the urge to be in the spotlight and just had to be seen. He knew the truth deep down, and the people closest to him would suffer. He hurt his wives and never gave his children what they needed. He has no contact or known relations to his children. This man is hurt, so he hurts everything in his reach. It is so difficult to see someone I love so broken. He tries to instill fear in others because he is afraid. He hurts others because he is hurt, and most importantly he wants others to suffer because he is suffering. The saying is true that "hurt people, hurt people."

Being the youngest of our family has been something that I have enjoyed thoroughly. I find myself making it very clear that I am the "baby" in the family. Like me, my older sister is always very clear about her in our sibling lineup. She demands respect, and finds herself always stepping in when I need her. Getting us together in a room is like creating magical chaos. My sister loves teaching others, and finds herself trying to bring everyone together. One thing about my sister is that she is stubborn as can be. When she has her mind made up, no one can change it. You see, looking back I can remember always having to voice that I understood what was happening around me. My sister thought that since I was the youngest that I do not remember things that our family went through. For instance, when I was younger my mom had a stroke. For some reason, my sister thought I would not recall this moment, but contrary to her belief I will remember this moment forever.

Unlike other people in our family, some siblings really try to make their feelings known. One of my sisters frequently calls and sends birthday gifts to my parents and other siblings. It is almost as if she is fighting for a position that she should already be given to her. Everyone has not made her feel welcomed, but I have always accepted her with open arms. Just like any other siblings, my sister and I have had a few disagreements but we have still made our way back to each other. When it comes to her, I give her the same truth that I give my other siblings because in my eyes I have no reason not to. Like all of us, she has her faults but is nevertheless a great big sister.

Losing a sibling is never easy, but thinking about all the memories that we created gets me through the heartache. My sister was a loving, caring and family-oriented person. When she loved, she loved hard. One thing about it is that she loved her children. They were her world and she deserved the world. When I found out my sister had cancer, I instantly began to find every resource to help her. I wanted to make sure that I did not lose her. Even in pain, my sister kept a smile on her face. She was always there for everyone else, but where were those same people when she was fighting cancer? I could not just let my sister go through this fight alone. Many may not know this, but I lost my sister and son around the same time. It gives me so much peace to know that my son is not alone. His auntie is there with him, and I know she will keep him out of trouble! I love you sister and I always will.

Even though I have experienced horrible things at the hands of my siblings, I still love them. You see, I have my shortcomings too, which I will speak on a little later. In order for this family to heal we have to start addressing our issues. It is just like the woman with the issue of blood from the bible. It was not the physical bleeding that caused her deficit, but it was actually her mind that was wounded. The woman felt that she had to touch the garment of Jesus to be healed, but what she did not know is that her healing was already done. She just needed to claim it. In her mind she had already had a vision of what healing would look like. It is all about how we think about things. Our minds have been programmed to hide our imperfections but what I have found is that God is not looking for perfection. He looks for those who have been stained but have a willingness to live for God. He does not use perfect people to reach imperfect people. In fact, he uses those who have been through the storm so that when they speak of his goodness they speak from experience. As a leader, when a situation arises that is not so great I challenge you to show the people who God is through your actions. Before moving on, I say to my siblings that I love you. My hope is that God helps you find peace. I hope one day that we can all come together. The time for love is now, and when the time is right we will come together...I just hope that we do not have to fall before we move forward.

So I got to thinking about the parallels to friendship. I hold friendship and sisterhood near my heart. What does it mean to have people who will really keep it real with you? It is very important to express to your friends and your loved ones why they are kept close and why you value their opinions. I don't have friends that I have not had around at least 10-20 years and the reason is I value their opinions, I value their acceptance and I value their corrections. If you cannot accept the chastising of a friend then what does that say about you. Do you think you are so perfect that you value nobody? I have watched this with my siblings. They don't have any friends and even friendships they have have been thrown away like they aren't important.

I watched my sister throw years of friendship away and she expected her siblings to also not talk to the person once she was finished with them. I would look at her in disbelief, a friendship that you've grown and nurtured for years, how is that so. As for my brother, he just doesn't have the pastoral friends that are like, "Look Doc…" Is there not even one person that he can look at as a friend to tell him that he should consider something different? The direction, the advice, the 'I am coming to you in love, as my friend, as my brother…' That is so disheartening. I can come to my friends and they come to me. They come to me because they refuse to see me fail but when we are so high and think so highly of ourselves and don't have that then I will tell you we are destined to fall. Our father sought wise counsel for so many people and that is why he had the success he did. I always clung to my parents for the direction I needed in life. They are still the best pattern. Thank you Lord for direction, thank you God for protection.

Chapter 5: Butterfly

Throughout the entirety of this book I have stressed that I am not perfect, and I could not complete this book without showing where God has brought me from. The love that I have for my son's father is indescribable, not because I want to be with him but because my son could not have come from anyone but him. He aided in the birth of my king. We were so young when we met, for me it was more than love at first sight, but I would say we had a connection that was unmatched. Our parents would become best friends and this added a deeper connection. Our mothers would shop together, his father was a deacon at our church who would be later called to preach. I was such a tomboy that I wanted to do what the boys were doing. My son's father wanted more but I started dating another guy who was a member of the church. He saw that I was into my son's father and he began to question the depth of our relationship. I would always tell him that he was more like a brother. Throughout everything, we were still best friends. The summer after my freshman year, we went on a church trip to Texas. All of the young members rode in one van, chaperoned of course. Robert sat next to me the entire ride, and it felt as if we were the only two there. I don't know what happened, but air and opportunity gave him the courage to grab my hand. It solidified how I felt for this man, and the rest of the trip we held hands and just talked. While on this trip we stayed up all night and we talked about everything. One night, I went to him with tear-filled eyes and told him, "I am not like the other girls, and I will not compete with them." He looked into my eyes and said, "I don't want you to, and I have always loved you." He asked me if a relationship is what I want, and if so, we can do this. My feelings forced me to tell him I wanted him for myself. His reassurance made me feel confident...more confident than I had ever felt.

We had to tell our parents, and we told his dad first, who drove the van that we rode in. I needed to tell my parents but they were old school; so old school that when I had my son my mom still was in denial that I had a boyfriend. We also had to go back to school where everyone assumed we were cousins. The people at school were shook when we walked in as a couple. We never told them we were related but our friendship was just that deep to where they just assumed. Nevertheless, we were in love and did not care what anyone thought. That was my man and I was his woman. Our first year was amazing, and we spent so much time together. He was everything to me and he had me on an emotional high. At such a young age, he just knew how to be present in every way.

We got a little touchy feely but we did not have sex in the first year. He was patient with me and he never pressured me into sex. I started paying attention to our surroundings and noticed that everyone was sexually active. I felt some type of way about that and decided it was time to talk about going to the next level. He was not a virgin and I started to think he is going to have sex with someone else if I don't do it. We talked about it and I told him that I was ready but I wanted it to be special. I planned it all out in my head. He asked several times if I was sure, and I was sure. When the night arrived, he covered more than all of the bases. The evening was beautiful. When the actual act happened, I was not prepared because that shit hurt like hell. He asked if I wanted to stop and I didn't want to. He was so understanding and held me while I cried. I was so distraught. That didn't last long, because we kept at it and we turned into nymphomaniacs. I was so young and not well versed in sex, and I now know more about my body.   To this day we laugh about how much we did not know back then. As time would progress, we had our shares of ups and downs. We broke up and got back together several times. My junior year, the inevitable happened, and I found out I was pregnant. He was happy, but I was in disarray. I found myself in a state of denial about the whole situation.

To buy some time, we decided not to say anything yet. He even told me to put ketchup on pads and put them in the trash so my mother would think I was still having periods. That plan didn't work for long! I was sleeping a lot more and missed the school bus often. My mother burst into my room one day and said, "Get your ass up, today is the day of reckoning! You are going to get a pregnancy test today!" I played the role like I didn't know why she was saying that. She told me to get dressed and she walked out. I was soooo scared. I snuck and called Robert to tell him and he asked if he should come. I said, "Hell naw nigga, if you come over now, she is going to kill you!" To make matters worse, she made my brother take us. We went to Planned Parenthood and when we got there I could not find words, and then the lady asked me about my last period. I played dumb of course and went to take the test. When they came with a pink slip saying it's positive, I said, "I told yall I was positive I wasn't pregnant."   The lady looked at me and asked me if I wanted to talk one on one and I said yes. She gave me all of my options but I already knew I was keeping my baby. I gave her the details and she gave me the due date of January 24, 1994. My mother being the person that she is, didn't talk down to me. She immediately went into protection mode and started doing what she knew was in the best interest for me and my unborn child. I remember when we got home, my brother ran to the phone and started telling everyone. I was humiliated and pissed at the same time! I felt like my mother and I should have gone alone so that I could be the one to tell my story. I first called my baby's father and confirmed what we already knew. He was and always will be a stand-up dude in my eyes.

I went into labor the day after Thanksgiving. I was thinking it was them damn chitterlings. My baby's father showed up with blue balloons thinking he was about to have a son. Due to all of the complications, I told the doctors that if it came down to me or the baby to save me. My son's father ran out the room and told the doctors to put me on suicide watch because of what I said. I never said I was going to kill myself; I just knew that I was young and I could not allow my child to be born without me being here to raise him. The doctor assured me that we would both be fine. They were able to stop my labor, and a couple of weeks later, I went into labor again and this time they could not stop it. I didn't call my baby's father because this was routine and I didn't think I was going to have the baby. My hesitancy to call him caused him to miss the birth.

When the baby came out, the doctor yelled out that he was a boy as if his ass forgot the whole time he said it was a girl. My momma said to the doctor, "I know you're a damn lie!!!" I'm not sure who called Robert's father, but someone did, and when he walked in he was HOT because he wasn't there for the birth. When he laid eyes on the baby, which to my surprise was a boy, all of his anger disappeared. When I notified my family and friends that I had the baby and it was a boy everyone thought I was pranking them. My son was born on December 12, 1993 at 5:22 am. He was 5 pounds, 6 ounces, and 19 inches long. I would be damned if that man was not right about what he felt. He was connected to his son well before he made his debut into the world.

Well, I was in utter disbelief because I knew I was about to have a girl. I had all girl clothes, a girl name, and it took a little bit to adjust to the fact that I now have this baby boy. He was absolutely perfect. From birth this boy had a way of softening the heart. I didn't care that he was a boy but what was

I going to name him? In my mind I knew what I wanted his name to be, and it was not going to be Robert. His name was going to be Darius Tyneal Theus. I had not solidified the name yet because his dad wanted him to be named after him, and I knew it would take some convincing to get him to agree with me. By this time, my friend had showed up and I began to drift off to sleep. While waiting for me to wake up they sat on the sofa while I rested.

Now listen to this shit! Before I went to sleep, the nurses referred to my baby as Baby Theus. When I woke up, I picked my baby up and I looked at the bracelet around his ankle and it read Robert in blue and white letters. I said, "What is this?" The nurse in her squeaky Mickey Mouse voice said, "It is the name that you picked and filled out on his paperwork." Mocking her I said, "No ma'am, I have not given you his name yet, and his name is Darius Tyneal." She let me know that I had already filled out the paperwork and that I might have been loopy from the medicine they gave me. I heard some laughter coming from the corner and my friend said, "His name is Robert Earl Theus V." I could have killed her! I later found out that they filled out the paperwork while I was asleep. I was at the highest level of pisstivity. The crazy ass nurse then proceeds to tell me that the only way I could change it is if I go down to City Hall. It was ordained, and his name was meant to be Robert. His father gave him to me and for that my love for the two Roberts will always be!

Chapter 6: Love is a Journey

"Love is patient, love is kind *and* is not jealous; love does not brag *and* is not arrogant, does not act unbecomingly; it does not seek its own, is not provoked, does not take into account a wrong *suffered*, does not rejoice in unrighteousness, but rejoices with the truth; bears all things, believes all things, hopes all things, endures all things."

—1 Corinthians: 4-7

THE CHURCH DIDN'T TEACH ME HOW TO LOVE. Instead the church taught me how to lie, cover up my lies and be as sneaky as possible. The church taught me to be perfect without ever showing me anyone who actually was perfect. The church taught me to run to marriage so I could have sex and have babies but not what it took to really make a relationship, let alone a marriage healthy and sustainable. I am grateful for the lessons of my parents but when I tell you I had to figure out so much on my own it was something else. We have to do something different and better for our future generations. The church is losing because it isn't being honest about the world we live in, regardless of where we worship.

We experience different types of love throughout our lifespan. I haven't had many relationships in my life. I now realize that I've only been in love two times. As I have gotten older I can differentiate love and infatuation. Love is supposed to be this beautiful thing, but I cannot explain what I felt in my marriage. You see, through the dark times I have always felt the presence of God and one of the darkest was in my marriage. My son's father was my first love and as important as Robert's dad was to me, he was not my husband. Before I tell you about Leon (oh my goodness this man made me realize what truelove really was) I have to tell you the things that led me to him.

Are you ready to enter the real world of lies, deceit and entanglement? Are you ready for Geneva to expose herself, not let herself off the hook, not silence her ill deeds and to get free doing so? If you are, buckle in!

I met Aaron through a cousin and he lived on this cousin's block. On paper he checked off as the perfect catch, no kids with a great work ethic and valued family. Much like my husband, Aaron was so intuitive to what I needed and he was always present in the moment. Our dates would just be amazing. I was just so smitten by him. We dated for four years with no relationship title. I had gotten away from Robert's dad who I donated 20 years of my life to. I wanted to date and Aaron gave me just that. He would make love to my soul and it was just what I needed. Now Aaron's behavior totally mimics my son's father who was such a gentle soul. Damn I hate that I took advantage of Robert's dad and I believe in many ways I ruined him for the next person. I think about how he was with me; he was so gangster, but with only me he was such a soft, loving, passionate person. Can you imagine what was about to happen —this hardcore, quick-tempered gangster and this rebellious, feisty, teenage girl? Both preachers' kids, were in love, having unprotected sex and would now give birth to a mix of all those traits.

To be truthful, I really do I think I made a horrible wife in my own marriage even though my ex-husband told me differently a million times. I believe Robert's dad's wife is the perfect specimen of a woman and she is and has always been perfect for him. My prayer is that she isn't paying for damage that I caused him in the past. There have been times where I've wanted to give spiritual advice to them about what could make their relationship better but I didn't know if she was ready to receive it. They are good people who deserve to love each other unconditionally.

As for me, I know I carried baggage from my relationship with Aaron into my marriage. I allowed Aaron to screw my brains out. He was a gentle spirit but he was not willing to give me what I wanted so I carried that through my courtship with my future husband. Aaron was the standard at that time and although I said YES, I knew my future husband was not what I truly wanted. Aaron and I would go on dates and even a few trips, but I wanted to BE with him and he couldn't offer that.

At the top of the year in 2003, I was in Louisiana for my baby cousin's birthday. Her house was THE party spot! There were always guys over. We went to the party. I was a hot item that night, the men were approaching left and right. A guy came over and said, "you aren't from here, you are very well put together. My friend wants to dance with you," "Are we children? Tell him that if he wants to dance he needs to ask," after 20 minutes he finally built up enough courage to come and ask me to dance but I told him I didn't want to dance to a fast song. He felt defeated. When another slow song came on he returned to shoot his shot once again. I told him that I was leaving. He didn't stop there, he asked if he could walk me to my car so I allowed him to.

We exchanged phone numbers after that we talked on the phone. For a few months day and night he was a great conversationalist. I couldn't remember what he looked like and I never looked him in the face. At this point it didn't matter, he had begun to sell me a dream. I loved him based on his voice and conversation. I told myself I would no longer go for the bad boy and I was going to go with what my Daddy alway presented when he would say, "One day you're gonna miss out on your husband, because you're too busy expecting Denzel when it's one eyed Willie who's gonna love and honor you". So I asked my friends if I should go meet him, after all, he offered to pay for everything. Everyone told me to follow my heart, no one said pray, simply follow your heart. So I went down and for the first time we met face to face again but I never looked him in his face. The anxiety that took place when I drove to his mom's house was something else. I remembered opening the door and laying my eyes on him. How had I not seen it? He had keloids all over his face. I thought I loved him based on our talks and immediately they didn't matter.

The weekend we spent together was perfect. He nailed it from my favorite foods, to flowers, opening doors, perfect conversation—I was sold. When it was time for me to leave I cried and shared with him the matters of my heart, I told him there was no way I could uproot my child and bring him to Lucky, LA. I also told him how attached I was to my parents at the time he worked for his pastor. He agreed to risk it all. He told me upfront that he would not make a move unless I was agreeing to marriage. This was when he dropped the first bomb that he had been married previously, they were together on paper for three years but their marriage only lasted 11 months. I told him he needed to have the divorce completed before he could move forward. Only one of the four children were his, he stated that the marriage was a bloody hell. The ex-wife was so disrespectful. She called the house all the time playing games and he never wanted to address her behavior.

So once again, without seeking spiritual counsel I made a big decision and I accepted his proposal. Now it was time to break this news to my family and the bigger problem was that I was not feeling the idea of us being engaged. However he only agreed to move if we were getting engaged and I would never let my parents down by shacking with a man from Louisiana after they preached this continually. At first it seemed like things were going to be good. He got hired at Wonder Bread and my son loved him. But the next shocker I was not prepared for. One night he came and laid his head in the middle of the bed and said, "I have a confession," my heart sank as he shared that he had been called to preach. The shit was starting to suck. WHY ME?? I didn't ask for this shit. I have had to be a preacher's kid. I damn sure didn't want to be a preacher's wife! For the first time I asked God why this was happening. I struggled so much during this time, I was trying my hardest not to fail at this, to support him in his vision but inside I felt like things were chaotic. What was happening? Why weren't the feelings of love present before we got married? I asked myself but ignored it until I broke down later.

Two months before my wedding I called Aaron and asked him, "do you love me," and with that voice that he always manages to charm my panties off with he replied, "Babygirl you know I love you.'. I went on to tell him, "I have two months until my wedding day if you tell me not to get married Aaron I promise I won't do it." "Baby girl you are so deserving of marriage. I would never tell you not to do that,". That wasn't the answer I wanted to hear.

Two weeks before my September wedding day I had the biggest emotional breakdown. I couldn't stop crying. My sister and my mother came to my house both reassuring me that what I was feeling was normal and that I should get married. I should have known better, all the signs were there. I just chose to ignore them and give myself what I felt I needed and not what God wanted me to have.

My soon to be husband preached his first sermon. He was a powerful preacher who would only study the night before and that was impressive. Even though I wasn't feeling him completely, I was torn about thinking about if I was missing a calling or if it would be brighter after awhile. There was a scripture to fit every occasion but I wasn't sure which one worked for me. So, I got married. After awhile, even when he preached well I couldn't hear his words anymore, I felt he was a hypocrite and then I knew it was over.

In my marriage there was never any physical or emotional abuse. My ex just was not that type, he was really mild mannered and very respectful. He just could not be faithful, hell after I found out he cheated I couldn't be faithful either. Nevertheless we stayed tied to each other in marriage for seven years. We put on a happy face for everyone but we were miserable, or at least I was. He didn't want the divorce at all. What hurt the most was that my idea of marriage was broken. I knew from my parents what marriage was supposed to look like.

When I found out about the incident I think I may have started to convince myself that maybe I would grow to love him. We were changing phone carriers and had to switch the sim cards over into the new phones. He was now working at Bayer and was not at home at the time. I activated all the phones and OH MY GOD...How could I have been so detached? I didn't see this before my eyes, I hadn't even kept up with his schedule. It all made sense this is why he was saying, "I know when you get out of school you are going to divorce me." As the phone kept updating there were more and more messages being transferred to the phone, I saw all these messages popping up and one particularly from this one woman. I became enraged seeing all the messages and I begin to think, "how the fuck are you cheating on me and you look like this." Oh the search was on. I found her address, packed all his shit and dumped it in her front yard. He was pissed and I told him he had to go.

From there my Dad wanted us to do counseling and I didn't want my Dad to do it. The pastor ripped him to shreds when I talked about what he did. One day this friend called me a bitch. We made it another two years and the cheating didn't stop. At this point I became this get back monster and I started saying to myself that if this is the marriage we had I was going to really show him. The shit he was doing could not even be compared to what I was doing. I was popping way more than he was slanging.

Aaron and I began meeting in the parks, hotels and I got into an emotional affair with a pastor who lived in California. It grew like a wildfire. I was feeling victorious because I knew everything he was doing and he knew nothing of what I was doing.

My husband was sleeping with not only the same woman I caught him with on the phone the first time but also one of my closest cousins. He was keeping his dogs behind her house and she came onto him and they had sex. We rarely had sex but this was the end of the journey. We stayed on this journey for another year and a half. I went to my cousin's house with a gun and he told her and she packed up her house and left. I didn't talk to her for about four years. In my heart I felt life would do more harm than I did. Her kids rebelled, sickness fell upon her. I HAD to forgive her and even with him I had to get out of it too. He wanted to stay because of the benefits to the family, not because he loved me.

I watched the show Cheaters all the time but one day I was leaving Aaron's sister's house and the sister stays right next door to my family member's house. We sat, talked, had wine and after we had sex I was leaving the house when the motion lights revealed me. I fell to the ground and I was sure the show Cheaters had caught my ass. My clothes were full of dirt and mud that night. I was so dirty, in more ways than one. I told myself that I had to end it. I was no longer doing it to hurt my husband, I was satisfying myself.

This last incident we had been to church on a Sunday and there was a prestigious family there. We hadn't seen the young son for a long time. When I was driving out of the parking lot, I told him, "boy, your ass ain't been to church in forever," and he told me that he would be coming back. As I parted ways with the young man Aaron called me and told me to meet him at our spot. I called my niece to cover for me like always. Aaron and I met in our secret place in the park, I left my phone in my car. This was the spot where we were caught by the police just a few weeks before. They knocked on the windows and told us we could go to jail but even that was not enough to stop me.

We would sit and talk, spend time together. When I got back in the car I had all these missed calls. The first one I looked at was from a woman in the church. I had all these voice messages from my husband and my niece. I decide to call my husband and he tells me that the young man, had been shot and killed. I knew at that moment I had to get out of my marriage. So I went and picked my mom up. She was so hysterical so by the time I got to her I told her that I would take her and we went up there with the family. I apologized to God and knew I had been doing the wrong thing. I knew it was God telling me to stop and make everything right. I ended it with Aaron that day.

When I filed for divorce, my husband started to stalk me and my son. I went to Bass Pro Shop and I bought a gun for protection. I walked out of my best friend's beauty salon late so my best friend's husband walked me to my car and saw my husband was waiting outside. I told my husband's mom and my dad and I started the paperwork and that he was behaving oddly. I think he was trying to shake me up about moving on but I wasn't having it. He didn't want to get the divorce and told me he wouldn't stop me. My Dad called him and told him that I would take him out and that he needed to leave me alone. The lawyer told me $3000 and I told a close friend about it and she told me I could do it myself for $133. The divorce was finalized, I sent the papers to his mom and I called her to tell her that I would take him out if he kept testing me. I think he heard his mother's voice of reason. We were divorced April 29, 2013 and he was married May 2, 2013. There is a woman out there who should be thanking me.

He married one of the many women he was cheating with. The one he is married to should know she would never have him if I didn't forge the name. When I told him I was writing this book I wanted to make peace. He said, " I am sorry, I did so much wrong to you and your family will have to come back to you," the Holy Spirit put things on his heart to share. This healing has helped me to want to love unconditionally and the desire not to ever want to be married is gone. He told me I was a phenomenal woman.

NEW DAY

Funny story. When Leon found out I was writing the book and I told him he would be in the book he said, "I am definitely suing you." I told him he was definitely a big part of why I am able to smile, why I am able to push through all the ugly stuff life has thrown me. You don't know why God puts people in your lives when you first meet them but over time you come to discover why. Then all of a sudden it hits you and you understand. He is my support. He is my reason to push through. Just everything that I have needed he has been there. It has been tough sometimes but breaking down the walls and the cells I had to really do with him. I would do it 100 times over because he is worth it. He has been here through the roughest part. When my son died, I yelled out, "why did you leave me, you knew I would not be ok," and on the third day my son came to me and said, *Mama, I left you because I knew you would be in good hands.* He would come to my son's room before he came to my room. When my baby came to me I knew I would be ok. Leon stayed at my place the entire year and one night He went to his home to grab some medicine and I told him to just stay there because he had just been there so much for me. Even then, I did not really spend the night alone because he stayed on the phone with me all night. He has truly been my rock.

When we first met I was going through my divorce I told my friend I would go to the Baptist Convention, her name is Quisha. Unfortunately, she passed away the same year as my son. She always called me MO-KAN-NE and had this loud, fun and boisterous voice.

"Girl, I got this man who I have been friends with since I was little. I know you are going to say no because you are going through a divorce but you have got to meet him, E."

"Qui, NO, I WANT TO BE A 'HO!" The truth was I really wanted to be alone, spend time with myself. I had even started taking myself to dinner and on dates.

"E, you know that is not you, you know you aren't built like that. I really want you to meet him, just do me a favor. He is already up there and just show him around and see what happens."

"Fine, I don't want to leave him in the land alone..."

Our first conversation was fine but I wanted to see what he looked like, that was the most important thing to me. I asked if he had Facebook and he said yes. He had a full beard, he needed a haircut and he was wearing a striped shirt (which I hate). I had every single reason to not like him. I had just moved out north of the river and I was certain to make him hate me so we would never meet again. My plan was to order a bunch of high cost shit and make him so annoyed that he wouldn't want to date me.

He gives me an address but it is only two blocks from my house. I had to quickly say, "let me call you back" and I realized I couldn't follow through with my plans because he was staying in the complex right next to mine. I can order all the food but I can't ghost him because we live so close to each other. I told him that we stayed in the same complex and he shared that North KC was safe and that was how he picked his apartment. So we settled on a date and I had double booked because I was going to hang out with my best friend Temeka at the casino. I knew I was on a time schedule. I went to pick him up and he asked which restaurant I wanted to go so I chose Outback Steakhouse. My plan to sabotage goes into motion. I am ordering lobster, steak, ahi tuna, just all kinds of shit. We had the best conversation! We meshed well and then I thought OH SHIT, this guy really has my attention. When dinner was over he didn't seem to be bothered that I had ordered so much food. As the date came to an end I had to acknowledge that my heart was feeling something. I remember pulling up to his house and not wanting the date to end. We kissed, and that kiss tied us together for ten years. If anyone would've told me this man was going to enter my life and help shape me into the woman that I am today, I would've never believed them.

Leon is a LEO, a true Leo, and it is like pulling teeth with him. Keep in mind I said to him I never wanted to be married and then after time I realized this is the man I actually desire to marry. He was there for me when it mattered most. When I found the most precious gift myself, and when I lost the most precious gift my baby. The truth was I had a messed up idea of love because I never was in love with my husband. He has never done anything crazy to me but he has definitely done some dumb shit. Like we had our own space together and when our lease was up and instead of finding a place first he ended the lease and to me that was super dumb. He is a more of a fly by night and I plan my every move to a T. He is that one person I can look at in the face and say, "What the fuck are you thinking," and now I feel like I want to be married and he is like, "no, you don't get to choose now,". He was once engaged and that relationship was long term and it just had too many holes in the relationship. He is stubborn and so was she. The marriage didn't happen but the baggage of that relationship came into ours and when I got it I was like AH-HA! I know he...I never wanted to hold hands or be spooned but he made me want to do all those things. He brought that out in me. He softened me in a way no one else never has. I am so grateful for that.

He was so used to me popping off and yelling but now I use my therapeutic voice. He was a little thrown off by all that was happening. The last barrier is that he is such a manly man. He will sit and struggle through things without telling me. He will never tell me he is in a hard way but I will tell him for sure. One of the big barriers is that he was so impatient. There were times I just didn't think I could stick it out. The last barrier is about him, relinquishing his trust. He has shown me through my hardest times that he is present for me but there is just nothing else to do but jump in and trust. Love conquers all!

He is such a riot to be around. You really have to be trusted before he lets you in. One of the things he has experienced is that family matters are family matters. He is blown away by the things that have occurred in the family. He has watched other men in the family speak of things that they shouldn't. He has spoken up when one of my brother-in-laws was disrespectful. He shared that he wasn't welcomed to return to stay in Tennessee with that behavior.

His job moved him to Tennessee and at first we were doing the long distance love then I just made the decision to go be with him. He had this belief that I didn't make the decision to go be with him and that my family had me in a hurtful place instead of me just wanting to come be with him but they could not be more wrong. Yes, he is a refuge for me but I definitely wasn't running to him to escape dealing with family. I actually wanted to be with him.

My son said he was going to go if I went. No one believed we would move but we did. I said I never wanted to be married because everyone else was choosing marriage for us. Now, I want us to choose it for ourselves. Would I like to get married, sure, and even yes, but I am also ok knowing how real and genuine the love we have is for each other. We have been able to have such special moments like traveling out of the country, going to dinner and drinking wine together. We are the opposite of what my marriage was. My ex-husband and I did so much with other couples and we were seen as a power couple but it was a lie.

Leon and I have such a genuine relationship of just living in the moment and our time together is just with us and is perfect. We don't spend time showering each other with material stuff to cover up the pain, lies or other discomfort, instead this is that put-your-toes-in-the-grass kind of love. It's that go out and just listen to good music kind of love. Even if we were to get married I would want a tattoo ring instead of a traditional ring because that will never come off and I think that is exactly the kind of love we have.

Initially my thoughts about Leon was that he didn't have any children so he wouldn't have the understanding about sacrificing for anyone but that's not true at all. We have separate places but I think it's working for us. When I was healing in the early part of grieving he really was doing everything for me. When I look back on it I was just a zombie and kind of existing. I was with him each and everyday and night, he was even driving me everywhere because I was afraid to drive. I would ask the question, "how do you feel like I am doing?" and he would tell me that he just didn't know. I could tell he was worried about me so I would have to tell him and show him that I was ok.

I would spend four hours in my son's room and he wasn't sure if I was ok or not. One day I was in the shower just crying for an hour. He told me that I needed to communicate or he would break down the door. I knew I had to do it one day, that I needed to conquer staying home. We made love and I was laying on his back and I told him that I was not going home when he left and I told him that I had to do it at some point. I had seen the cardinal (which I think is Robert) and I told him that I would be ok. He told me he wasn't sure if I can handle it and rightfully so. Out of the blue I decided to just drive home by myself, I didn't tell him I was going to do it I just called once I got on the highway. I know he was probably afraid for me but he knew I had to do it too. He checked on me often, told me to keep my music on and I did just that. Praying all the way there. I just had to do for myself but it was nice to know I had his love and support.

This man has seen me at my worst and at my best. My son never took on too many men, but he loved him. I don't know what our future will hold, but I do know to publicly give flowers where they are due! Thank you for loving me when I was unlovable. Thank you for being a father figure to my children, and thank you for being Paw Paw to my grandbabies.

Chapter 7: Address it!

I have come to realize why I have been a little unpopular in some ways. One part of being a preacher's kid really is about turning a blind eye to the dysfunction that can be happening in our own families. I no longer value this nor subscribe to this. My belief is to make it known that when something happens we should address it, out loud, right then and there. Too often I feel when I address it I am addressing it by myself. No one else addresses whatever the issues are so when I say something, the fault, the drama, the pain all falls on me as if I created it. This would often leave me feeling really defeated and asking myself why did I open my mouth in the first place. I would even think it was some kind of punishment but I now know this isn't true at all. God said to just speak it!

There is a concept called neutrality that we can gain all access to. It is the thing that says, you don't have to involve yourself in everything. Take the option to not be in shit. For instance, one of my siblings needs to take this position a lot of the time. There are some things that are going to work itself out. We don't have to take sides and you don't have to be in the middle of it. I am looking at the dumb asses in my family and just look and see, no one wants to be in the middle of this, and we can stay NEUTRAL. Everyone is not going to handle situations the same but how hard is this shit? Ain't everybody gonna handle shit with integrity and morals. I just wish that more people could consider what is actually fair. They could learn how to depersonalize situations.

There is a point in saying something even if you think it is not going to change. Not saying something doesn't help either. Are we going to stay in these unhealthy places and not get anything solved or anything done? Do you think something is going to get solved by being quiet? A closed mouth don't get fed. Problems don't get solved by just sitting back and being quiet. We need family meetings that put it all on the table and where everyone has a voice. To whom much is given, much is required. When God gives a family a task and you think you can just keep going and rolling around in mess that is NOT ordained by God. God doesn't want us to be a horror show. We are supposed to be a blessing to no longer be in or of disorder and chaos. That's where the black Christian family has failed. If we read the word we see the Bible uses the messiest person to show how God really works. We want to make it where we are all clean and holy and can't make a mistake. That's why the worldly people say we are nothing but hot drama soup. We act like we can't make a mistake because it makes us look so stupid. I know God said, "He who hasn't sinned cast the first stone," yet many church families act like we are sitting on a throne and can't do wrong. I want to break down my family and you tell me, which one of my siblings do you want to pattern after? We are all wretched and undone but are acting like we are on a throne.

Everyone of us, when we have family dinner...Daddy says, "I have three kids I can count on and one went on to glory...The father, son and holy ghost, the trinity." Me, a sister and another sister out of his ten children see about him. Neutrality is to accept your role in how we have helped our parents and grandparents. The children need to be neutral when their parents haven't done what they should be doing for our elders.

I have learned to let God handle the man of God when he is wrong. I had to learn for myself even when the man of God is wrong, he DOES need to be corrected. He needs to be told. So at some point even the man of God has to be told he isn't right but it has to be told in a spirit of love. Even though I don't see eye to eye with my brother I had to tell my sister, don't disrespect our brother. I never disrespected him on Facebook; I went to his defense and have had his back. I have watched all this unfold and then I knew God ordained me to speak up. The Spirit touched me.

I told my brother I supported him financially, I haven't disrespected him and he knew I was right. He couldn't say a word. Every time we have had family dinner I am the one planning it. Now others made sure it was together but my two sisters, if they planned the dinner it would be crazy. Every time we had a falling out, I was the one who tried to get the family back together. I told them we needed a potluck and to get together as a family and we welcomed absent family members back. I started to realize if I don't come out and say let's get together as a family it doesn't happen. At all. I will be honest, I have done it forever and I am not going to do it again until the spirit tells me its time. That is when I move now. I keep seeing on Facebook that the elders of this family don't think we are united. They are asking me what I think we should do. I believe if Robert was here none of this would be happening. He was looked down on but he kept the family together but these so called ministers of the family don't have enough sense to know that. We have to stop playing church. We've got to stop. We've got to stop! We need to be kneeling at the altar ourselves.

Chapter 8: My Journey

I have told you all about my life at this point. I have shared my flaws, my family, and even the hardest moments of my life. You see, this book is dedicated to my baby so it needs to end on a good note. There will be no more talk of lies, deceit, or anything negative. There will only be talk of growth, healing, and hope. My journey was for a reason, but at the time I was blinded by depression, anxiety, and sadness. It was not until I asked God to remove those things from my mind that I was able to break out of my bondage. God was sending me all of the signs, but my mind had been overtaken by all the negativity. So, the calmness you see now, just know, I had to pray and ask God for it. The peace of mind and smile on my face you see, just know I had to work for it.

I think the saddest thing of all is that some people act like they don't know what it feels like to be confused or sad. I know what it is like to experience sorrow, I know what that is like to feel alone, I know the pain of suffering and being inoculated. I know what it's like to have things pan out and then go the total opposite way. The feeling of being misguided, sad, mad at the world, I know it all. It's ok. Have that feeling for a second, a minute, an hour, a day or even a month but do not let it consume you because you are a fighter, you are strong. I think that is what destroys those most who seek to destroy your image or make you want to feel down all the time, when they know you won't let it overtake your life, when you won't let grief get the best of you. Grief was a part of my life but it was not my life. It did not become a permanent part of my life. I choose to love, I choose to accept that loss was a part of my life and to allow it to only be a moment of my life.

As I think back, I can't help but think of the moment everything came together. It was the exciting Kansas City Chiefs versus Denver Broncos game. I wanted to go but I was not sure if I was going to buy tickets to the game. To my surprise, my bonus daughter surprised me with tickets. For some reason, the spirit told me to purchase an expensive Denver Broncos shirt to give to someone at the game. Like a faithful servant I vowed to do just that. I got a shirt made for me that said, "repping my home team and repping my angel". Anyone who knew my son would know that he loved the Broncos. Myself on the other hand, identifies as a die hard Chiefs fan. When we got to the game we realized that my knucklehead of a daughter purchased tickets in all Denver territory. I told myself that I could just cheer for both teams. When the Chiefs scored I would cheer at the top of my lungs. The Bronco fans around me would look at me and frown every time. The looks that this particular lady gave me when she turned around sent chills down my spine. She was not a nice lady and normally I would be ready to fight. I wanted to just sit down and stay quiet, but I heard God say, "Stay the course my child." After confirmation, I continued to cheer, but now with a bit more confidence. At that moment I heard God say, "Give her the shirt." The lady's yelling was interrupted by me tapping her on the shoulder and she turned around and yelled, "WHAT?" and I quickly handed her the shirt. She said, "for me" and I said, "yes, I wanted to give you a gift." I explained to her about losing Robert to explain why I was cheering for both teams. Her anger vanished in the blink of an eye. She thought I was coming to her in anger, but I came in peace. After my explanation and with tears in her eyes she apologized and thanked me all in the same breath. She told me that she thought I was going to yell at her and hit her and I said, "why would I do that?" I knew my task was complete and began to leave the stadium.

Robert and I would always taunt each other during these rivalry games. When I left the stadium the Chiefs were losing and then I heard the crowd erupt. The Chiefs had scored the last three seconds of the game. I heard a whisper in my ear, like it was touching my ear and the voice said, "ha ha Mama, they were going to win all along..." I was immediately filled with emotion and lost it in more ways than one.

After leaving the game, I had finally realized what God was trying to tell me. While at the game I was surrounded by people, yet I was all alone. When I wanted to give up, God wanted to see if I could trust in him and remain steadfast. I was able to follow through with the task that God had given me. It was almost as if I heard God whispering to me, "You are ready!" To prepare me for my calling God had to isolate me, I was not ready to step into my calling and God knew that. He knew what I lacked and nourished my mind and spirit. So, today I announce to you the new me. What others had tried to take, God gave back to me tenfold. I have a new walk, a new talk, and a restored mind. I have run for years, but God has shown me that all roads will lead back to him. Thank you Lord for your unmerited favor that continues to cover me.

Can we come together as a family? Do we continue to make everyone seem like everything is ok? Do we keep putting up posts for social media without ever reaching out to the people who are impacted the most? I know this is my story, but this is a lot of black families. We have to have outside mediators who can be neutral, who can stand for the unity of the entire family and help us unravel the pain. *Iyanla, Fix My Life*, is a real show for a reason. I know that I am willing to do our healing work. I will never stop loving my family but I will no longer condone bad behavior, sexism, addiction and more. My hope is that seeing this book in black and white will help us all to hold the mirror up to ourselves, including myself. No, I am not a pastor but I will share the word of God. There was not a platform in place, but I was able to create my own, and most importantly I have let go of things that have tried to destroy me. I can now say, I am strong. I am free. I have laid my burdens down.

About the Author

Geneva N. Rambo is from Kansas City, Missouri and currently lives in Tennessee. When she isn't working as a school counselor she is leading Bible Study, spending time with her granddaughters and traveling. Geneva plans to work on her next book in the coming year. For booking contact geneva.rambo@gmail.com

Made in the USA
Middletown, DE
20 February 2024

49465487R00046